Pink Panther™ Cocktail Party

PINK PANTHER™
Cocktail Party

ADAM ROCKE

Pink Panther™ 40th Anniversary
Illustrations by **SHAG**

This edition published in 2005 by
Virgin Books Ltd
Thames Wharf Studios
Rainville Road
London
W6 9HA

PINK PANTHER™ COCKTAIL PARTY is
published in USA by Surrey Books.

Pink Panther 40th Anniversary illustrations
 by Shag
Designed and typeset by Joan Sommers
 Design, Chicago
Printed and bound in China by Imago

5 4 3 2 1

ISBN 1-85227-294-5

A catalogue record for this book is available
from the British Library

Contents

Introduction

MIX ONE PART CARY GRANT, ADD A SHOT OF James Dean, and garnish with a pinch of Jerry Lewis. Blend them together and what have you got? One of the smoothest and most sophisticated cartoon characters ever to prance across the screen.

Part movie star and part menace, the Pink Panther turns 40 this year. To celebrate his coming of age, raise your glass and invite some cool cats over to your Pantherland Lounge. If you're not as smooth and suave as he is, you certainly will be after tossing back a few of these dandy drinks. The hip and funky feline-type tippler can paw through libations like the *Red Devil* and the *Yellow Rattler* from Pink on the Wild Side. If you're a more curmudgeonly cat, the Classic Pink drinks will suit your laid-back lifestyle.

There's nothing like a charmingly inept host to enliven a party, so treat your guests to Inspector Clouseau's inimitably sly style. Plop on a fake nose, trip over a table leg (preferably with lots of glassware in hand), and adjust your accent accordingly: Make sure everybody in the "rheum" has their drinks "rahfresh-ed." To keep you from bumbling your way through the bar, we've added all the helpful drink-mixing hints you'll need to be as clever as Cato.

Until we meet again, this party is sol-ved. . . .

Setting up your "Pink" bar

Utensils

A properly outfitted "Pink" bar will contain these essential items:

CAN and BOTTLE OPENERS

CORKSCREW (the new air-powered "pump" varieties are excellent)

CUTTING BOARD (wooden or synthetic)

ICE BUCKET (with plenty of ice!)

ICE CREAM SCOOPER

ICE TONGS/ICE SCOOPER

JUICER (aka JUICE EXTRACTOR)

KNIVES (any small set; make sure a PARING KNIFE is included)

LEMON/LIME SQUEEZER

MEASURING SET (includes various-sized cups and spoons)

MINIATURE UMBRELLAS (an absolute must!)

MIXING GLASS

MIXING STICK (aka MUDDLER; usually wooden)

NAPKINS (cocktail and, for goblet-sized drinks, dinner)

PITCHERS (for measuring and/or serving)

PLASTIC STRAWS (cocktail and long)

SHAKER SET (consisting of a metal tumbler and a
   mixing glass)

SPOONS (teaspoons and tablespoons, if not in
   Measuring Set)

STRAINER (two: medium and very fine mesh)

SWIZZLE STICKS (pink, naturally!)

TOOTHPICKS (for garnishes)

TOWELS or RAGS (for cleaning purposes)

Glasses

Your glassware shouldn't dictate the drink. Virtually any
libation can be served in any type of glass. But here's what
we suggest:

CHAMPAGNE SAUCER For wine or champagne.
Usually about 4 ounces.

COCKTAIL There are a wide variety of
cocktail glasses on the market, ranging
anywhere from 3 to 6 ounces with varying
sizes in between (such as $3^{1}/_{2}$, $4^{1}/_{2}$, $4^{3}/_{4}$,
etc.). Again, personal taste will dictate, but,
if possible, it's always nice to have two sizes
(at least) on hand.

COLLINS Multiple-ingredient drinks
are usually served in Collins glasses, as
are many "juice" and "cola" drinks. They
range from 10 to about 14 ounces, and
there are some, called TALL COLLINS, that
can hold as much as 16 ounces.

DOUBLE ROCKS (also called DOUBLES) For "rocks" drinks, these range from 12 to 16 ounces.

GOBLET Again, there are a wide variety of goblets. Beer goblets are traditionally 12 ounces, whereas other types can range from 10 to 14 ounces.

HIGHBALL A very common glass, these range from 8 to 12 ounces.

HURRICANE Excellent for two-person exotic drinks, this huge goblet is usually 22 ounces. However, we have seen some in "Island" bars that were as big as 30 ounces!

MARTINI These V-shaped glasses, usually in the 4 to 5-ounce range, are perhaps the most famous of the lot.

OLD FASHIONED (also called LOW-BALL or ROCKS) Very common glasses in the 6 to 8-ounce range. BIG/DOUBLE OLD FASHIONED holds 2 to 4 ounces more.

SOUR (also called WHISKEY SOUR or DELMONICO or GO-GO) While it can be used for a wide array of drinks, it most commonly houses sours. They range from 5 to 6 ounces.

Measurements

Here's a little chart to make sure all your pours are accurate:

1 cup	8 ounces
1 split	6.3 ounces
1 wineglass	4 ounces
1 jigger	1 ½ ounces
1 pony	1 ounce
1 tablespoon (tbsp.)	⅜ ounce
1 teaspoon (tsp.)	⅓ tablespoon
1 dash	¹⁄₃₂ ounce

Bottle Sizes of Wines & Spirits

When you do your shopping, these are the measurements you'll encounter since the liquor industry went to the metric system a few years ago. In the U.S. we often still use the old inexact designations:

Label size	Old U.S. designation
3 l	double magnum
1¾ l	half gallon
1½ l	magnum
1 l	quart
750 ml	fifth
500 ml	pint
375 ml	half bottle
200 ml	half pint
187 ml	split
50 ml	miniature

Mixers, Garnishes, and Assorted "Extras"

Stocking your "Pink" bar is a matter of personal taste, but here are some suggestions for items to keep on hand:

Bitters— orange and angostura are the two most popular varieties

Bloody Mary mix, pina colada mix, sour mix

Cinnamon sticks, sugar cane swizzle sticks, or any other "flavored" swizzle sticks

Club soda, seltzer, tonic water

Coffee

Cola, ginger ale, 7-Up or Sprite

Cream — light and heavy

Cream of coconut

Grenadine — made from pomegranates, this sweet, colorful (red) flavoring will see a lot of use

Ice — and plenty of it

Ice cream and sherbet

Juices — apple, cranberry, grapefruit, lemon, lime, orange, pineapple. Other "exotic" juices and nectars (kiwi, star fruit, mango, etc.) are available

Lemons, limes, oranges, pineapples

Maraschino cherries

Milk

Mint leaves — a "must have" for mojitos

Nutmeg

Olives and pearl onions

Rock candy syrup — can be substituted for sugar or used to add a touch of sweetness to any recipe

Rose's lime juice — differs from fresh lime juice because it contains a sugar-based syrup

Salt and pepper

Sugar — white granulated sugar and brown sugar are used most often

Tabasco sauce and Worcestershire sauce

Water — avoid using tap water in drinks

Liquor Glossary

Any well-stocked bar should prove more than adequate for a "Pink" bar. Depending on your personal tastes and budget, here's a basic rundown of what's out there:

ABISANTE — Pale green liqueur similar in flavor to anisette (licorice).

ADVOKAAT — Eggnog-flavored liqueur.

ALE — Bitter-tasting lager.

AMARETTO — Almond-flavored liqueur.

AMER PICON — A French combination of quinine, gentian, and oranges.

ANISETTE — Also called ANISE; licorice-flavored liqueur.

ARMAGNAC — Similar to cognac but only distilled once.

BAILEY'S — Irish cream liqueur.

BANANA LIQUEUR — Also called CRÈME DE BANANA.

BENEDICTINE — A liqueur made by the French Benedictine monks.

BLACKBERRY LIQUEUR — Like other "fruit" liqueurs, this cordial has the distinct flavor of its namesake.

BLENDED WHISKEY — Different whiskeys combined (called "married") in the casks.

BOURBON WHISKEY — Aged for at least two years in white oak casks and made mainly from corn.

BRANDY — Basically, the fermented juice of fruit. Comes in many varieties: cherry, blackberry, apricot, etc.

CANADIAN WHISKEY — Made from rye, barley, and corn.

CHAMBORD — A French liqueur with a very distinct sweet raspberry taste.

CHAMBRAISE — Another sweet French liqueur, this one is made from wild strawberries.

CHARTREUSE — Two types, yellow and green, created in France by Carthusian monks.

CHERRY HEERING — A cherry-flavored liqueur.

COGNAC — Fine brandy from France's Cognac region.

COINTREAU — Orange-flavored liqueur made from curaçao oranges.

CRÈME LIQUEURS — Many flavors, such as CRÈME DE CACAO (light and dark), CRÈME DE MENTHE (white and green), CRÈME DE CASSIS, and others, all with a creamy consistency and sweet taste.

CURAÇAO — Orange-flavored liqueur that can be blue or orange.

DRAMBUIE — A malt whiskey-based liqueur with a relatively sweet taste.

DUBONNET — A sweet-spicy French aperitif.

FRAISES — Strawberry-flavored liqueur.

FRAMBOISE — Another raspberry-flavored liqueur.

FRANGELICO — Italian hazelnut-flavored liqueur.

GALLIANO — Yellow-gold Italian liqueur made from various herbs and spices.

GIN — Liquor distilled from rye and other grains and flavored with juniper berries.

GRAND MARNIER — French orange-flavored, cognac-based liqueur.

IRISH MIST — Irish whiskey-based liqueur with the added flavor of oranges and honey.

IRISH WHISKEY — Of the whiskeys, the only one distilled three times.

KAHLUA — Mexican coffee-flavored liqueur.

KIRSCHWASSER — Also called KIRSCH; a black cherry-flavored liqueur.

KÜMMEL — Colorless liqueur flavored with caraway seeds.

LILLET — Red or white French aperitif wine.

MALIBU RUM — Coconut-flavored rum.

MARASCHINO LIQUEUR — Almond- and cherry-flavored liqueur.

METAXA — Greek brandy.

OUZO — Licorice-flavored Greek aperitif.

PEANUT LOLITA — Peanut-flavored liqueur.

PEPPERMINT SCHNAPPS — Mint-flavored liqueur.

PERNOD — Another licorice-flavored liqueur.

RUM — Liquor distilled from fermented sugar cane or molasses.

RYE WHISKEY — Made mainly from rye.

SABRA — Israeli orange-chocolate liqueur.

SAMBUCA — Italian licorice-flavored liqueur.

SCOTCH WHISKEY — Made from grain and malt; blended and single malt.

SLOE GIN — Made from sloe berries soaked in gin.

SOUTHERN COMFORT — Liqueur made by combining peaches, peach liqueur, and bourbon.

STRAIGHT WHISKEY — Made with one type of barley malt.

STREGA — Another sweet Italian liqueur.

TEQUILA — Mexican liquor distilled from the sap (fermented) of the mezcal plant.

TIA MARIA — Jamaican coffee-flavored liqueur.

TRIPLE SEC — Another orange-flavored liqueur.

TUACA — Italian citrus-flavored, brandy-based liqueur.

VANDERMINT — Dutch mint-chocolate-flavored liqueur.

VERMOUTH — Either dry or sweet, this aperitif wine is flavored with various herbs.

VODKA — Colorless liquor distilled from rye, wheat, or other grain.

WILD TURKEY — Bourbon-based liqueur.

WINE — Fermented grape juice.

YUKON JACK — Canadian whiskey-based liqueur.

Helpful Hints

Just a few helpful mixology hints:

1. Unless you're pouring the ingredients directly into the glass they'll be served in, use a mixing glass, or cocktail shaker, and keep your strainer nearby. Not only does this look better, it usually results in better tasting cocktails as the ingredients will have been combined more thoroughly. However, some drinks are supposed to be stirred, not shaken, so pay close attention to the recipe.

2. Never *completely* fill a mixing glass/cocktail shaker with ice. Half to three-quarters is plenty. Otherwise, when you

pour your concoction into the serving glass, it might over-flow. Base your ice usage on the size of the serving glass.

3. Unless it is otherwise specified, *always*, *always*, *always* chill a cocktail glass before serving a drink in it. This can be done by: a) filling it with ice cubes while you mix the drink, b) filling it with ice water while you mix the drink, or c) refrigerating it for 30–60 minutes before using it.

4. To fill a glass with ice, *never* dip the glass into the ice bucket. Always bring the ice to the glass by means of a scoop, preferably one made of metal or hard plastic. Ditto for putting ice in a blender.

5. To frost a glass with salt or sugar, first use a lemon or lime wedge to moisten the rim of the glass; then dip the rim into a saucer filled with the salt or sugar. Be careful not to press too hard, especially with glasses that have a thin edge. To frost with ice, dip the rim of the glass in water, then place in a freezer for 30–45 minutes. For frosting beer mugs, dip the entire mug in water.

6. Use fresh fruits and/or juices in place of canned ingre-dients and mixes whenever possible.

7. To float a liqueur (or any ingredient), slowly pour the ingredient to be "floated" over the underside of a teaspoon or a fat swizzle stick. The "float" will remain on the top.

8. Always add the garnish last *unless* a drink is being flamed.

9. To flame a drink, first float the substance to be ignited—usually grain alcohol or 151-proof rum—then light with a long match or long-nosed safety lighter. Be sure to keep paper goods, drapery, and eyebrows away from the flame.

Congratulations!
You're ready to begin mixing.

CATO

3 oz. plum wine
1 oz. crème de cassis
4 oz. 7-Up or Sprite

Cocktail; pour over ice, fill with 7-Up, stir. Cherry garnish.

COLONEL SHARKY

1 oz. light rum
1 oz. Amaretto
3 oz. guava or papaya juice
3 oz. orange juice

Cocktail; shake with ice, strain over ice. Orange slice garnish.

CLOUSEAU

¾ oz. bourbon
¾ oz. cherry liqueur
1 tsp. triple sec
1 oz. light cream

Cocktail; shake with ice, strain. Cherry garnish.

INSPECTOR DREYFUS

1½ oz. bourbon
½ oz. sloe gin
1 tbsp. sugar syrup
1 tbsp. cherry syrup
4 oz. orange juice

Cocktail; shake with ice, pour. Cherry garnish.

NUEVO CLOUSEAU

1 oz. blackberry brandy
¾ oz. lemon-flavored vodka
1 tbsp. lemon juice
1 tbsp. orange juice

Cocktail; shake with ice, strain over ice. Cherry garnish.

PHANTOM

(aka Sir Charles Cocktail)

1½ oz. lemon-flavored vodka
½ oz. triple sec
6 oz. grapefruit juice
½ fresh lemon

Cocktail; shake with ice, strain over ice. Squeeze ½ lemon but do not stir. Cherry garnish.

PINK PANTHER

(original)

¾ oz. gin
¾ oz. dry vermouth
½ oz. crème de cassis
½ oz. orange juice
1 egg white

Cocktail; shake with ice, strain.

PINK PANTHER COOLER

1 oz. Malibu rum
1 oz. Alize
6–8 oz. pink lemonade

Collins; shake with ice, strain over ice. Lemon wedge and cherry garnish.

PONTON

1 oz. vodka
1 oz. blue Curaçao
1 tbsp. Grand Marnier
4 oz. orange juice

Cocktail; shake with ice, strain over ice. Cherry garnish.

SIMONE'S CHAMPAGNE SHOOTER

4 oz. chilled pink champagne
4 oz. orange juice
1 tsp. crème de noyaux

Champagne saucer; shake with ice, strain.

XANIA

½ oz. Amaretto
½ oz. dark crème de cacao
2 oz. cream

Champagne saucer; shake with ice, strain. Cherry garnish.

Straight Up
Pink

Cocktails
with
a blush

PINK CADILLAC

1 oz. Chambord
½ oz. white crème de cacao
½ oz. Galliano
1 oz. light cream

Highball; shake with ice, strain over ice.

PINK CREAM FIZZ

2 oz. gin
1 oz. light cream
1 oz. lemon juice
1 tbsp. grenadine
1 tsp. sugar
4 oz. club soda

Collins; shake with ice, strain over ice. Fill with soda. Double cherry garnish.

PINK FLAMINGO

1½ oz. gin
¾ oz. apricot brandy
1 tbsp. grenadine
1 tsp. lime juice

Cocktail; shake with ice, strain.

PINK LADY

1 oz. gin
1 oz. cream
½ oz. grenadine

Cocktail; shake with ice, strain.

PINK SLUSH

1 oz. citrus-flavored vodka
   (lemon/orange/lime)
1/2 tsp. lime juice
4 oz. cranberry juice
Crushed ice

Champagne saucer; blend until
smooth. Cherry garnish.

PINK LEMONADE COOLER

1 1/2 oz. raspberry-flavored
   vodka
1 tsp. lemon juice
8 oz. pink lemonade

Tall Collins; fill with ice, add ingredients, stir. Lemon slice garnish.

PINK SQUIRREL

1/2 oz. white crème de cacao
1/2 oz. crème de noyaux
2 oz. light cream

Cocktail; shake with ice, strain.

PINKOLADA

1 1/2 oz. Chambord
1 oz. cream of coconut
2–3 oz. pineapple chunks
   (fresh or canned)
2–3 oz. pineapple juice
2 tbsp. strawberry syrup
1 tbsp. light cream
3 oz. crushed ice

Goblet; blend until smooth.
Garnish with strawberry.

FROZEN DAIQUIRI

2 oz. light rum
1½ oz. lime juice
1 tsp. sugar

Champagne Saucer; blend ingredients with 4–5 oz. crushed ice. Pour and serve.

(Use other fruits and corresponding liqueurs for FROZEN FRUIT DAIQUIRIS. Example: 1–2 bananas and 1 oz. banana liqueur for a FROZEN BANANA DAIQUIRI)

FROZEN MARGARITA

1½ oz. tequila
½ oz. triple sec
1 oz. sour mix
1–2 dashes Rose's lime juice

Goblet/Margarita Glass; blend ingredients with 4–5 oz. crushed ice. Pour and serve.

(Use fruit and corresponding liqueur for FROZEN FRUIT MARGARITAS)

FROZEN PINK PANTHER

1 oz. strawberry schnapps
1 oz. banana liqueur
1 oz. Malibu rum
2 oz. orange juice
½ oz. grenadine
Crushed ice

Cocktail; blend until smooth. Cherry garnish.

ICEBALL

1 ½ oz. gin
1 oz. white crème de menthe
¾ oz. Sambuca
3 tsp. cream
3 oz. crushed ice

Goblet; blend until smooth
and pour.

PIÑA COLADA

1 ½ oz. light rum
1 oz. cream of coconut
2–3 oz. pineapple chunks
  (fresh or canned)
2–3 oz. pineapple juice
1 tsp. light cream
3 oz. crushed ice

Goblet; blend until smooth.
Garnish with cherry and
pineapple wedge.

Pink on the Wild Side

BAY BREEZE

1 ½ oz. vodka
1 oz. cranberry juice
4 oz. pineapple juice

Highball; pour over ice, stir.

For MALIBU BAY BREEZE,
use Malibu rum.

CHI-CHI

1 oz. light rum
½ oz. blackberry brandy
Pineapple juice

Highball; pour over ice,
fill with pineapple juice, stir.

COSMOPOLITAN

1¼ oz. citrus-flavored vodka
¼ oz. triple sec (or Cointreau)
¼ oz. lime juice
1½–2 oz. cranberry juice

Martini; shake with ice, strain.
Garnish with lime slice or
lime twist.

GEISHA

2 oz. bourbon
1 oz. sake
2 tsp. sugar syrup
1½ tsp. lemon juice

Old Fashioned; shake with ice,
strain over ice. Cherry garnish.

JELLY BEAN

1 oz. Anisette
1 oz. blackberry brandy

Old Fashioned; pour over ice, stir.

JOLLY ROGER

1 oz. dark rum
1 oz. banana liqueur
2 oz. lemon juice

Old Fashioned; shake with ice,
strain over ice. Cherry garnish.

KAMIKAZE

1 oz. vodka
1 oz. triple sec
1 oz. lime juice

Old Fashioned; shake with ice, strain over ice.

MELON BALL

1 oz. vodka
½ oz. Midori melon liqueur
5 oz. orange juice

Highball; pour over ice, stir.

MOJITO

1 lime
10–12 fresh mint leaves
1 tbsp. rock candy syrup
1½–2 oz. light rum
2 oz. club soda

Collins; juice ½ the lime into a cocktail shaker, cut remaining ½ lime into quarters, add to shaker. Add mint leaves and syrup, crush with muddler to extraxt flavor. Add rum, club soda, and ice. Shake well and pour into Collins glass. Garnish with mint sprig and lime wedge.

PANCHO VILLA

1 oz. light rum
1 oz. gin
½ oz. apricot brandy
1 tsp. cherry brandy
½ tsp. pineapple juice

Old Fashioned; shake with ice, strain over ice. Cherry garnish.

RED DEVIL

½ oz. sloe gin
½ oz. vodka
½ oz. Southern Comfort
½ oz. triple sec
½ oz. banana liqueur
1 tbsp. Rose's lime juice
2 oz. orange juice

Collins; shake with ice, strain over ice. Cherry garnish.

SLOE COMFORTABLE SCREW

½ oz. sloe gin
½ oz. Southern Comfort
½ oz. vodka
Orange juice

Old Fashioned; pour ingredients over ice, fill with orange juice, stir. Orange slice garnish.

WOO WOO

¾ oz. vodka
¾ oz. peach schnapps
3 oz. cranberry juice

Highball; pour over ice, stir.

YELLOW RATTLER

1 oz. dry vermouth
1 oz. sweet vermouth
1 oz. gin
3 oz. orange juice

Collins; shake with ice, strain over ice.

Classic
Pink

AMERICANO

1 oz. Campari
1 oz. sweet vermouth
3 oz. club soda

Highball; pour over ice, stir.
Add club soda, stir.

B & B

½ oz. Benedictine
½ oz. brandy

Pony; pour Benedictine,
float brandy.

BELLINI

Peach puree or peach nectar
Brut champagne

Champagne Glass; pour peach
nectar, add champagne.

BLACK RUSSIAN

2 oz. vodka
1 oz. Kahlua

Old Fashioned; pour over ice, stir.

BOCCI BALL

1 1/2 oz. Amaretto
6 oz. orange juice
Club soda

Highball; pour over ice, stir.
Splash club soda.

BLOODY MARY

1 1/2 oz. vodka
3 oz. tomato juice
1/2 oz. lemon juice
2–3 drops Tabasco sauce
2–3 drops Worcestershire
  sauce
1 dash each salt and pepper

Collins; shake with ice, pour.
Garnish with lemon/lime slice
and/or celery stalk.

BRANDY ALEXANDER

1/2 oz. white crème de cacao
1/2 oz. brandy
1/2 oz. heavy cream
Nutmeg

Cocktail (or Snifter); shake with
ice, strain over ice. Dust with
nutmeg.

CUBA LIBRE

1–1 ½ oz. rum
Cola

Highball; pour over ice, fill with cola, stir. Lime wedge garnish.

DAIQUIRI

2 oz. light rum
1 oz. lime juice
1 tsp. sugar

Cocktail; shake with ice, strain. Lime slice garnish.

DORADO

2 oz. tequila
1 oz. lemon juice
1 tbsp. honey

Highball; shake with ice, strain over ice.

FRENCH CONNECTION

2 oz. brandy
1 oz. Amaretto

Old Fashioned; pour over ice, stir.

GIN AND TONIC

2 oz. gin
Tonic water

Highball; pour gin over ice, fill with tonic water, stir. Lime wedge garnish.

HARVEY WALLBANGER

1 oz. vodka
Orange juice
2 tsp. Galliano

Highball; pour vodka over ice, fill with orange juice. Float Galliano.

MANHATTAN

1 ½ oz. blended whiskey
½ oz. sweet vermouth

Cocktail; shake with ice, strain.
Cherry garnish. DRY MANHATTAN,
use dry vermouth and garnish with
an olive. PERFECT MANHATTAN,
use ¼ oz. of both dry and sweet
vermouth and garnish with a
lemon twist.

MARTINI

1 ½ oz. gin
¼–⅛ oz. dry vermouth

Martini; stir with ice, strain. Olive
garnish. Substitute vodka for a
VODKA MARTINI.

NEGRONI

1 oz. gin
1 oz. Campari
1 oz. sweet vermouth

Cocktail; pour over ice, stir, strain. Lemon twist garnish.

ROB ROY

1 ½ oz. scotch
¼–½ oz. sweet vermouth

Old Fashioned; pour over ice, stir. Cherry garnish. For DRY ROB ROY, use dry vermouth and garnish with an olive. For PERFFCT ROB ROY, use ¼ oz. of both sweet and dry vermouth and garnish with a lemon twist.

RUSTY NAIL

2 oz. scotch
1 oz. Drambuie

Old Fashioned; pour over ice, stir.

SEVEN AND SEVEN

1 ½–2 oz. Seagram's 7 Crown
  blended whiskey
7-Up

Highball; pour over ice, stir. Cherry garnish.

TOM COLLINS

1 oz. gin
2 oz. sour mix
Club soda

Collins; pour over ice, fill with
club soda, stir. Cherry garnish.

WHISKEY SOUR

1 oz. whiskey
2 oz. sour mix

Sour Glass; shake with ice, strain.
Cherry garnish.

WHITE RUSSIAN

1 ½ oz. vodka
1 ½ oz. Kahlua
½ oz. light cream

Old Fashioned; pour over ice,
float cream.

ALLEGHENY COCKTAIL

1 oz. bourbon
1 oz. dry vermouth
1 1/2 tsp. blackberry brandy
1 1/2 tsp. lemon juice

Cocktail; shake with ice, strain.
Lemon twist garnish.

EL SALVADOR

1 1/2 oz. light rum
1 oz. Frangelico
1/2 oz. lime juice
1 tsp. grenadine
1 tsp. lemon juice

Old Fashioned; shake with ice,
strain over ice.

FLORIDA PUNCH

1 1/2 oz. dark rum
1/2 oz. brandy
1 oz. grapefruit juice
1 oz. orange juice

Highball; shake with ice, strain
over crushed ice. Orange slice
garnish.

GOLDEN CADILLAC

2 oz. Galliano
1 oz. white crème de cacao
1 oz. light cream

Highball; shake with ice, strain over ice.

GRASSHOPPER

1 oz. green crème de menthe
1 oz. white crème de cacao
1 oz. light cream

Cocktail, shake with ice, strain.

HURRICANE

1 oz. light rum
1 oz. gold rum
1/2 oz. passion fruit syrup
1/2 oz. fresh lime juice

Cocktail; shake with ice, strain.

MAI TAI

1 oz. light rum
1/2 oz. triple sec
1/2 oz. orgeat syrup
1 1/2 oz. sour mix

Collins; shake with ice, strain over ice. Cherry and orange slice garnish.

PANAMA

1 oz. dark rum
½ oz. white crème de cacao
½ oz. cream
Nutmeg

Old Fashioned; shake with ice,
strain over ice. Dust with nutmeg.

PARISIAN

¾ oz. gin
¾ oz. dry vermouth
¾ oz. crème de cassis

Cocktail; shake with ice, strain.

SCORPION

2 oz. light rum
1 oz. brandy
2 oz. orange juice
½ oz. lemon juice
½ oz. crème de noyaux
3 oz. crushed ice

Highball; blend until smooth.
Orange slice garnish.

ZOMBIE

1 oz. light rum
½ oz. triple sec
½ oz. crème de noyaux
1½ oz. sour mix
1½ oz. orange juice
1 tbsp. 151-proof rum

Collins; shake with ice, strain over ice. Float 151-proof rum. Cherry garnish.

TEQUILA SUNRISE

1½ oz. tequila
2–3 dashes lime juice
2 drops lemon juice
Orange juice
½ oz. grenadine

Highball; pour tequila, lime, and lemon juice over ice. Fill with o.j. Add grenadine.

TRADE WINDS

2 oz. gold rum
½ oz. plum brandy
½ oz. lime juice
1 tbsp. sugar syrup
3 oz. crushed ice

Wine Glass (or Goblet); blend until smooth, pour. Pineapple slice garnish.

CALIFORNIA SUNSET

4 oz. chilled champagne
4 oz. pineapple juice
½ oz. cherry brandy

Cocktail; pour champagne, add pineapple juice, float cherry brandy.

CATACLYSMIC

1 ½ oz. gin
1 tbsp. grenadine
1 tsp. Rose's lime juice
7-Up or Sprite

Old Fashioned; pour ingredients over ice, fill with 7-Up/Sprite. Cherry garnish.

CAT & FIDDLE

1 oz. gold rum
1 oz. Captain Morgan's
   Spiced Rum
3 oz. orange juice

Old Fashioned; shake with ice,
strain over ice. Orange slice
garnish.

CAT'S EYE

1½ gin
¾ oz. green Chartreuse
½ oz. dry vermouth

Highball; shake with ice, strain
over ice. Orange peel garnish.

ELECTRIC PINK BANANA

5 oz. pink lemonade
1 oz. crème de banana
½ oz. melon liqueur

Old Fashioned; pour pink
lemonade over ice, add crème de
banana, stir. Float melon liqueur.

KITTEN CABOODLE

1 oz. Amaretto
1 oz. white crème de menthe
2 oz. crushed ice

Cocktail; blend until smooth,
pour. Cherry garnish.

MORNING WHISKERS

1 oz. bourbon
¾ oz. dark crème de cacao
½ oz. cream

Highball; shake with ice, strain over ice.

NINE LIVES

½ oz. dark rum
½ oz. dry vermouth
½ oz. gin
½ oz. light rum
½ oz. sloe gin
½ oz. triple sec
½ oz. vodka
½ oz. whiskey
6 oz. cola or Hawaiian Punch

Collins; shake with ice, strain over ice. Cherry and orange slice garnish.

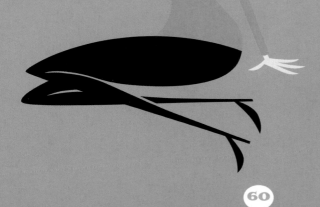

PANTHER POWER PROTEIN SHAKE
(non-alcoholic)

4 oz. low-fat or non-fat milk
2–3 oz. non-alcoholic eggnog
3 oz. protein powder
1 tbsp. chocolate syrup
1 tsp. vanilla extract

Goblet; blend at high speed, strain.

PANTHER'S RAGE

1 ½ oz. raspberry-flavored rum
1 can Red Bull
1 tsp. lemon juice

Old Fashioned; shake with ice, strain over ice.

PANTHER'S TAIL

1 oz. blackberry brandy
¾ oz. papaya juice
¾ oz. apricot nectar
1 tsp. orgeat syrup

Cocktail; shake with ice, strain. Add one "dimpled" ice cube. Fill dimple with orgeat syrup.

PINK DIAMOND

1 ½ oz. vanilla-flavored rum
½ oz. Curaçao
4 oz. pink grapefruit juice

Old Fashioned; shake with ice, strain over ice. Cherry garnish.

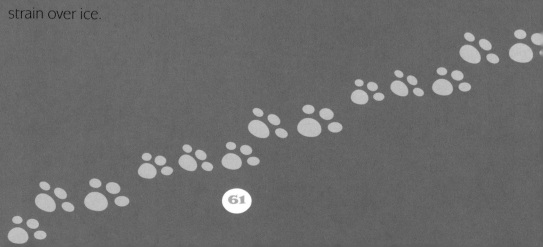